Contact after adoption

A longitudinal study of adopted young people and their adoptive parents and birth relatives

Elsbeth Neil, Mary Beek and Emma Ward

Published by British Association for Adoption & Fostering
(BAAF)
Saffron House
6-10 Kirby Street
London EC1N 8TS
www.baaf.org.uk

Charity registration 275689 (England and Wales) and SC039337 (Scotland)

© Elsbeth Neil, Mary Beek and Emma Ward, 2014

British Library Cataloguing in Publication Data. A catalogue record for this book is available from the British Library

ISBN 978 1 910039 13 7

Project management by Shaila Shah, Director of Publications, BAAF
Designed and typeset by Helen Joubert Design
Printed in Great Britain by The Lavenham Press

All rights reserved. Apart from any fair dealing for the purposes of research or private study, or criticism or review, as permitted under the Copyright, Designs and Patents Act 1988, this publication may not be reproduced, stored in a retrieval system, or transmitted in any form or by any means, without the prior written permission of the publishers.

The moral right of the authors has been asserted in accordance with the Copyright, Designs and Patents Act 1988.

BAAF is the leading UK-wide membership organisation for all those concerned with adoption, fostering and child care issues.

Contents

Foreword by John Simmonds	v
Introduction	1
Time 1: the preschool years	2
Time 2: middle childhood	4
Time 3: follow-up in late adolescence	6
The adopted young people: how were they getting on in adolescence?	8
The adoptive families: what contact was taking place with birth relatives?	12
Adoptive families' experiences of direct contact	14
Adoptive families' experiences of indirect contact	17
The satisfaction of young people with their contact arrangements	19
The adoptive families: adoption communication openness	22
Young people's perspectives on adoption communication openness	24
Being adopted: young people's construction of an adoptive identity	25
Birth relatives: well-being and adjustment to the adoption, 16 years on	28
The birth relatives: contact pathways and experiences	31
Social networking websites: new challenges for adoptive parents, birth relatives and adopted young people	35
Summary of findings and practice implications	37
Publications from earlier stages of the study	41

Acknowledgements

We would like to thank the Nuffield Foundation for funding the research. We would also like to thank the local authorities and voluntary adoption agencies which have helped us with this research; we are particularly grateful for the help of After Adoption, which assisted us in recruiting a group of adopted young people to advise us about the best ways to encourage adopted young people to take part in the study, and of course to the young people who took part in this reference group. Thanks are also due to the academic experts, adoption professionals, and experts by experience who formed our advisory group, and also to our academic colleagues, both within and outside of the University of East Anglia, who gave us advice and carried out a rigorous review of our report. Most of all, we would like to thank all the adopted young people, adoptive parents and birth relatives who have taken part in this study over the years for their willingness to give up their time and share their personal experiences.

About the Nuffield Foundation

The Nuffield Foundation is an endowed charitable trust that aims to improve social well-being in the widest sense. It funds research and innovation in education and social policy and also works to build capacity in education, science and social science research. The Nuffield Foundation has funded this project, but the views expressed are those of the authors and not necessarily those of the Foundation. More information is available at www.nuffieldfoundation.org.

The authors

Elsbeth Neil is a Senior Lecturer in Social Work and Director of Research in the School of Social Work at the University of East Anglia. She has a degree in Psychology from the University of Leicester, and a Master's degree and PhD in Social Work from the University of East Anglia. She is a registered social worker. Elsbeth began this study in 1996, and has directed all three stages. She has also carried out research (as part of the Adoption Research Initiative) exploring support services for birth relatives in adoption, and support for direct post-adoption contact arrangements.

Mary Beek has a degree in Applied Social Studies from the University of Bradford, and a Master's degree in Social Work (by Research) and a PhD from the University of East Anglia. Mary is a registered social worker and is currently working as a professional adviser for Care for Children, where her role is to facilitate the training of foster carers for children in the Far East. Mary's career in social work spans over 30 years and she has worked primarily in adoption and fostering. For many years she has combined practice with research and writing, and has worked as a researcher on several UEA projects in the field of family placement. She is co-author with Gillian Schofield of the "Secure Base" model of training for foster carers and adoptive parents.

Emma Ward has a degree in Psychosocial Sciences and a PhD in Social Work, both from the University of East Anglia. Her doctoral research looked at adoptive parent motivation. Since completing her PhD, Emma has worked as a researcher on a wide range of projects at UEA including studies of permanency in foster care, the experiences of parents of looked after children, and looked after children and offending.

Foreword

There have always been questions about "what works" in adoption. These questions have not always focused on the same issues – the debates that led to the Adoption of Children Act 1926 focused on the turbulence following World War I and a major flu epidemic where children were placed in alternative family arrangements with no legal security or scrutiny. "Baby farming" was one serious issue but concerns about the inheritance of the moral failings of the birth parents being passed on to the "adoptive parents" through the child and then influencing their social standing in society was a very significant concern. Secrecy became a powerful and important part of the solution, with the notion of adoption being a "new start", unencumbered by anything from the past.

Secrecy came to play a dominant part in adoption until the 1960s and 70s. But in the years that followed, information about origins, the integration of the past into the present and the formation of an adoption identity for the children and adults emerged as powerful themes. This included the possibility of actual relationships between adopted people and their birth parents – a theme powerfully encapsulated in Mike Leigh's 1996 film, *Secrets and Lies*. That argument has largely been won, but this is not to underestimate the complexity, sensitivity and emotional nature of this "coming together" of the past with the present and the immediacy of the network of possible relationships that comes with adoption.

These issues have taken on a new form over the last 25 years, during which adoption in the UK has mostly focused on the placement of maltreated rather than "illegitimate" children. Knowledge about and an identity based on "real time" experience and relationships through contact is an important part of the adoption solution. But questions continue to be raised about the impact on children's development and, indeed, recovery from abuse and neglect when the "realities" and explanations of what really happened are sorely challenging to "put into words" and make sense of. Contact is a solution but it may also become a threat and in some circumstances a serious one.

The Contact after Adoption study is groundbreaking in its approach to these questions for both policy and practice. For a research team to have the commitment, perseverance and opportunity to start their study in the pre-school years, continue through middle childhood and end in late adolescence is remarkable. To have the skills, knowledge and expertise to manage what they discovered is also remarkable. The University of East Anglia team demonstrate all in abundance.

The study makes a major contribution to these ongoing questions of "what works in adoption". It reinforces the ways in which adoption must be seen as a family life over time, and a family life that struggles with challenging questions and powerful emotions alongside the routines, liveliness and resourcefulness that enable this. Adoptive parents and birth parents clearly play their part in this, but above all it is the young people themselves that drive this research story. And in adoption, that is as it should always be.

John Simmonds
Director of Policy, Research and Development, BAAF

Introduction

Since the introduction of the Adoption and Children Act 2002 in England, and corresponding legislation in Wales and Scotland, contact between an adopted child and his or her birth relatives must be considered and discussed in the child's placement plan, although there is no duty to promote birth family contact. The key consideration when deciding about contact should be the child's welfare throughout their life. It is important therefore to have an understanding of how contact affects adopted children, not just in the early days of the placement, but also as they grow and become adults themselves.

Existing research evidence about contact after adoption has found that the impact and quality of post-adoption contact can vary widely. In some cases, contact is wanted and valued by children; it can facilitate the maintenance of important relationships and meet identity needs. But in other cases, contact has been found to unsettle or disturb children, especially where there is a history of abuse or neglect between the child and the birth relative they are having contact with. There is very little research that has included the views of adopted teenagers and young people, particularly in situations when children are adopted from care.

This study has followed up a group of adopted children (all placed under the age of four) and their adoptive parents and birth relatives, where some form of post-adoption contact was planned between the child and adult birth relatives. The key aims of the study were to explore people's experiences of contact and the impact of contact on the children and adults.

The adopted young people followed up in this study were placed for adoption in the mid to late 1990s. This was a time when agencies were a few years into a period of experimentation with more open adoption arrangements; the potential drawbacks of closed adoption were known, and the possible benefits of open arrangements were being considered. The families living with these more open adoption arrangements, such as those who have taken part in this study, are to some extent pioneers in that they have attempted more open arrangements in the absence of a strong body of evidence about the impact of open adoption on adopted children, adoptive parents and birth relatives, particularly for children adopted from the care system.

The study has been carried out in three stages:

- **Time 1 at the preschool age**;
- **Time 2 in middle childhood**; and
- **Time 3 in late adolescence**.

This summary report very briefly outlines findings from the first two stages of the research, before highlighting in more detail key findings from Time 3.

Names and identifying information have been changed.

Time 1: the preschool years

What did we do?

- This stage of the project took place from 1996–2000.

- Questionnaires asking for detailed, non-identifying information were sent to the social workers of all children adopted or placed for adoption from mid-1996–1997 across 10 adoption agencies. Questionnaires about 168 children were returned (a 90 per cent response rate).

- Interviews were carried out with adoptive parents and birth relatives involved in face-to-face post-adoption contact arrangements. Thirty adoptive families (who had adopted 35 children) took part, as did 19 adult birth relatives (including 12 birth parents) from 15 birth families. These interviews took place, on average, two years after the child's placement for adoption.

Key findings from the survey

- The most common form of contact planned for children was agency-mediated letterbox contact. Such contact was planned for 81 per cent of children, and usually this contact was to happen once or twice a year.

- Only 11 per cent of children had a "closed" adoption where no ongoing contact was planned.

- All types of contact mainly involved birth mothers and/or maternal grandparents or siblings. Fewer than 30 per cent of children had a plan for any contact with their birth father or his relatives.

- Face-to-face contact with adult birth relatives was planned much less frequently than letterbox contact – in only 17 per cent of cases. Nine per cent had a plan for face-to-face contact with a birth parent.

- Where face-to-face contact was planned, this was usually in cases where children were adopted from care. Children relinquished as babies were unlikely to have this kind of open adoption, even though their birth parents had far fewer personal difficulties than the parents of children placed from care.

- Wide variations in contact planning between different agencies were found, suggesting that decisions were often being made according to agency values or culture rather than a consideration of each case.

Key findings from the interviews

- Contact arrangements were in some cases frequent, informal and took place at the home of the adoptive parents or the birth relatives. More usually, contact was infrequent (once or twice a year), taking place either in a public place or in a supervised setting.

- The most helpful approach by agencies seemed to be one that supported and empowered families to find an arrangement that worked for them, rather than dictating a standard approach.

- Face-to-face contact, even at high levels, was not found to get in the way of the development of the relationship between the adoptive parents and the child.

- Because this group of children had been placed early and had often not lived with their birth parents for very long, they generally did not have close relationships with birth relatives at the time of placement. Most children, because of their age, had only a very limited understanding of adoption. This meant that for children contact meetings were not emotionally charged and were generally accepted easily and often enjoyed by them.

- In some cases where contact was quite frequent, a relatively close relationship with the birth relative could develop. More often, however, children were said to enjoy visits (especially when friendly attention and gifts were involved) but their adoptive parents felt that they were too young to fully understand the significance of the meetings.

> **He is fairly excited because he knows he is going to get a present and he is going to play in the sandpit...not necessarily because it is his birth mother but because of the whole event.**

Most adoptive parents showed high levels of empathy for the child and empathy for the birth relatives. This could mean that adoptive parents who have such qualities are more likely to agree to open adoption arrangements. But there were also ways in which contact seemed to help adoptive parents develop empathy. For example, negative fantasies about the birth family could be challenged by actually getting to know them. Contact could also eliminate fears that birth relatives could threaten their relationship with the child. In some cases, contact reassured adoptive parents that adopting their child had been the right decision.

> **I did feel quite nervous about direct contact. I suppose it is quite threatening, that worry that there is going to be that genetic thing – that your daughter is going to see this person once a year and suddenly love them and you are going to be out of the picture...but there wasn't at all. It was just somebody nice who was playing with her.**

- An open and empathic attitude on the part of the adoptive parents was the factor most closely related to whether or not contact continued or increased.

- Almost all the birth relatives really valued being able to see the child.

- Three-quarters of birth relatives had reached a position of accepting the adoption and were realistic about their current and future role in their child's life. This was possible when birth relatives had not agreed with or wanted the adoption. Some birth relatives did not fully understand or accept how their role differed from that of the adoptive parents.

- This position of acceptance and support for the adoptive parents was frequently one that developed over time as birth relatives felt reassured that the child was well and that the adoptive parents were nice people.

Time 2: middle childhood

What did we do?

- This stage of the project was carried out from 2002–2004, seven years (on average) after the children were placed for adoption. It was funded by the Nuffield Foundation.

- Most of the families included at Time 1 took part again. New families who had a plan for indirect contact between the child and an adult birth relative were also included, most of these being found from the original cohort of 168 children.

- Sixty-two adoptive families (with 87 adopted children – we included adopted siblings as well as the "target" child) took part; 43 adopted children from these families were interviewed. Seventy-two birth relatives from 62 different birth families were also interviewed. Birth relatives and adoptive parents also completed some questionnaires.

Key findings

- Almost all the children who were interviewed felt that they were loved and that they belonged in their adoptive family. This was true regardless of their contact arrangements with birth relatives.

- Some children experienced problems outside the family (usually at school) related to teasing about being adopted.

- Children in this study did not yet have a full understanding of adoption. Many children were curious about their birth family. A wide range of feelings about being adopted and about birth relatives (both positive and negative) were expressed.

- Children generally accepted whatever contact they had (which ranged from none to frequent face-to-face meetings) as normal and ordinary, and very few children wanted anything that was particularly different to what was in place. Children involved in ongoing contact arrangements generally valued the contact. If they expressed any dissatisfaction, this was usually related to contact that was not happening, e.g. when birth relatives did not reply to contact letters or if they had stopped coming to meetings.

> I would like birth mum to get in touch with me and I would like [my brother's] adoptive parents to let us know a bit of information, receive phone calls from them 'cause we don't even know what his voice sounds like. (Amanda, age 11; letters sent to birth mother, but no replies received)

- The majority of children were doing well in terms of their emotional and behavioural development, but 31 per cent (23 of 74) had emotional or behavioural problems that were clinically significant. Children who had problems in these areas tended to be those who were older at placement and had more difficult backgrounds in terms of experiencing maltreatment and/or changes in their main caregiver.

- No significant differences were found between children who had face-to-face contact and those who did not in terms of their emotional and behavioural development. Neither did the openness of adoptive parents relate to children's emotional and behavioural development.

- Adoptive parent satisfaction with face-to-face contact was generally high, with adoptive parents usually reporting that this contact was either positive or neutral/unproblematic for their child. They often described meetings as being low-key and like seeing a distant relative.

- Adoptive parent satisfaction with indirect contact was more mixed, with many adoptive parents finding letters hard to write and finding the response (or lack of response) from birth relatives disappointing. Children were not necessarily being included in letter contact.

- Adoptive parents varied in terms of their Adoption Communication Openness (ACO), i.e. how open they were to talking and thinking about adoption, their comfort with the child's connection to their birth family, and their empathy with the perspectives of the child and birth relatives. Adoptive parents having face-to-face contact had significantly higher ACO scores than those having indirect contact.

- About half of the birth relatives had accepted the adoption and supported the adoptive parents. The remaining birth relatives were either resigned or angry. Grandparents were more likely to show positive acceptance than birth parents, and birth relatives involved in face-to-face contact were also more likely to show positive acceptance compared with those who had no face-to-face contact.

- Almost all the birth relatives felt that having any form of contact was better than having no contact. However, contact could be a very mixed experience – some birth parents did not keep up meetings or respond to letters for both practical and emotional reasons.

- Contact plans made at the time of placement had often changed in the years following adoption and both increases and decreases in contact were found.

- Both face-to-face and indirect contact worked best where both the adoptive parents and birth relatives could empathise with each other, think about the child's needs, and relate to each other in a constructive and collaborative way.

- Where indirect contact was planned, a one-off meeting between the adoptive parents and birth relatives was usually highly valued by both parties, and increased the chances that indirect contact would be sustained over the years.

Time 3: follow-up in late adolescence

What did we do?

This stage of the project (also funded by the Nuffield Foundation) explored six key research questions and aimed to draw out implications for practice.

- How were the adopted young people getting on in terms of their emotional and behavioural development, perceived well-being and relationships with their adoptive parents?

- What types of openness had adopted young people, adoptive parents and birth relatives experienced since the last follow-up?

- What were the views of adopted young people, adoptive parents and birth relatives about the contact plans they had experienced?

- How were the adopted young people making sense of their adoptive identity?

- How open were adoptive parents in talking and thinking about adoption with their child?

- How well were birth relatives doing in terms of their mental health and their acceptance of adoption?

Who took part?

We were able to locate almost all of the 62 adoptive families who had taken part at Time 2; 45 families agreed to take part again (73% of those who had been in the study at Time 2). Adoptive families who stayed in the study were no different from the families who dropped out in terms of the children's histories and their emotional and behavioural problems in middle childhood. They were, however, more likely to have been having face-to-face contact at Time 2 and their adoption communication openness scores were higher compared with the parents who dropped out of the study.

In 43 of the 45 families who took part, one or both of the adoptive parents were interviewed (39 adoptive mothers and nine adoptive fathers; couples were interviewed together). In two adoptive families, the adopted young person took part but their adoptive parents did not. The adoptive families were mostly married couples at the time they adopted; four adoptive parents were single adopters. At this third stage, seven couples had divorced and three adoptive parents had died.

The 45 adoptive families had adopted 65 young people who were part of the study. There were slightly more males (n=38) than females (n=27). The young people were aged 13 to 22 with an average age of 18-and-a-half years. Three-quarters of the young people were in the 17–20 age range. Three young people were of dual heritage, the remainder were white British/European. Their age at placement ranged from 0 to 52 months with an average age of 21 months. Most children (n=45, 69%) had been adopted from the care system. Fourteen children (21.5%) had been placed by their parents in complex cases, for example, because of the child's disability, because a parent was struggling to cope, or because the child was rejected. Six children (9.2%) had been relinquished at birth by their parent/s.

Adoptive parents were asked to pass on to their children invitations to take part in the study; some adoptive parents felt it was not appropriate for their son or daughter to take part because they were having problems, or because their child had a learning disability that limited their communication. Forty adopted young people agreed to take part; 32 were interviewed and eight young people decided only to complete the questionnaires.

Birth relatives were harder to track down than adoptive parents; in some cases they were not found, or had died. Thirty-seven birth relatives took part, 52 per cent of those who took part at Time 2. Almost half of the birth relatives interviewed were grandparents (18 of 37), a third were birth mothers (12), and five were birth fathers. The sample also included an aunt and an adult sibling. Thirty-four birth relatives were white British/European and three were of dual heritage. More birth parents had dropped out of the study compared with grandparents and five birth parents were known to have died since the last follow-up. Birth relatives who remained in the study in general had fewer mental health problems and were more likely to have shown acceptance of the adoption at Time 2 compared with birth relatives who did not take part.

Methods

Families were invited to take part in a face-to-face or telephone interview, depending on their preference. Individuals were also asked to complete some questionnaires.

Adopted young people

- The interviews focused on their experiences of contact; their satisfaction with contact; their views about adoptive family communication about adoption; their adoptive identity; and their ideas for improving contact practice. The interviews included some brief activities to help young people to focus on the questions.

- Young people were asked to complete five questionnaires looking at: emotional stability; views of self; overall life satisfaction; relationships with adoptive parents; and adoptive parents' communication about adoption.

Adoptive parents

- The interviews explored events in the family since the last interview; the young person's development and progress; communication about adoption; contact with birth relatives over the last 10 years; views about contact; and suggestions for improving contact practice.

- Adoptive parents were asked to complete a measure about the young person's emotional and behavioural development.

Birth relatives

- The interviews asked about life events since the last interview; contact with the adopted child and their views about this contact; feelings about the child's adoption; and suggestions for improving contact practice.

- Birth relatives were asked to complete a questionnaire about mental health/psychological well-being.

A mixture of qualitative and quantitative methods was used to analyse the collected information. When carrying out quantitative analysis, checks were made as to whether it was appropriate to run statistical tests. For some analysis, statistics were not used because the sample was too small to pick up even large differences. Where research findings are referred to as being "significant", this relates to where a statistical test was used and the results showed that any differences or correlations found were highly unlikely to have occurred by chance.

The adopted young people: how were they getting on in adolescence?

Emotional and behavioural development

The adoptive parents of 46 young people completed a measure of emotional and behavioural development (the Child Behaviour Checklist, or the Adult Behaviour Checklist for those over 18). We looked at whether young people's scores were in the normal range, or whether their scores showed they had problems (scores in the borderline or clinically significant range).

- Forty-eight per cent of young people had internalising problems.
- Forty-three per cent of young people had externalising problems.
- Compared to Time 2, more young people had internalising and externalising problems.
- Pre-placement risks (history of abuse, caregiving changes, age at placement) were significantly associated with higher levels of externalising problems in adolescence.

Life satisfaction

- Thirty-nine young people scored themselves on a life satisfaction ladder where a score of one indicated "the worst possible life for me" and a score of 10 indicated "the best possible life for me".
- The average score on this measure was eight, and over three-quarters of young people (23) scored themselves at seven or higher, suggesting high life satisfaction.
- Six young people scored themselves at five or six, suggesting they were struggling with their life satisfaction.
- Three young people scored themselves below five, indicating that they were currently very dissatisfied with their lives.

Emotional stability/instability

- Thirty-six young people completed the General Health Questionnaire, which looks at how people see their current mental well-being and whether they feel better or worse than usual in relation to a number of symptoms. Young people who said they felt worse than usual on three or more of the 12 items were considered to be currently emotionally unstable.
- Ten young people (27%) had scores in the emotionally unstable range.

Self-liking and self-competence

- Thirty-six young people filled in the Revised Self-Liking and Self-Competence scale.
- The mean score of young people on this measure was similar to that found in a large sample of university undergraduates.

Relationships with adoptive parents

- Thirty-six adopted young people completed the Inventory of Parent and Peer Attachment. This asks young people to rate how they feel about their parents in terms of mutual trust, quality of communication, and extent of anger and alienation.
- The large majority of the adopted young people perceived their relationship with their parents as being generally positive.
- Ninety-four per cent of young people had very high scores (in the top quarter of the available range) when rating their relationship with their mother, as did 88 per cent of young people when rating their father.

Overall ratings of young people's progress

Using all the information we had about the young people, we developed ratings of their overall progress. We identified three groups of young people, and were able to categorise 63 of the 65 young people into these groups.

The thriving group

Young people in the thriving group appeared not to have any significant problems in their life. They seemed happy and emotionally stable and had good relationships with their adoptive parents. They had a range of abilities, but all were engaged positively in education, employment, training or voluntary work and many had a range of interests or hobbies they enjoyed pursuing. Of the 32 young people in this group, exactly half were male and half female. They were on average 18 years old. Sixty-one per cent had been adopted from the care system. A substantial minority of young people (43%) had a low pre-placement risk score, indicating that they had not experienced much adversity such as abuse or neglect or frequent changes of caregiver. However, some young people in this group did have a difficult background, but nevertheless were doing very well, their development often having improved over the years.

> **Jacob was placed for adoption at three-and-a-half. He took a long time to settle in his new family, and in middle childhood he was having a lot of problems in school. By late adolescence he was doing really well academically, socially and in terms of his relationship with his parents.**

The surviving group

Young people in the surviving group were doing well in some areas of their lives, but all had ongoing difficulties causing moderate concern in at least one area. Several of these young people had been through a very difficult time earlier on, and were now becoming more stable.

> **Luke was placed at three years old. The most difficult time for him seemed to be in primary school where he found it hard to get on with the other children; he was bullied and his behaviour was difficult. At home he showed signs of both anger and separation anxiety in his relationship with his parents. By age 19 Luke had made a lot of progress; his peer relationships had improved and he was doing quite well in terms of work and education. He still found getting on with other people difficult at times, and his feelings of anger towards his adoptive mother continued to surface occasionally.**

The young people's overall progress

Thriving (51%)	Surviving (29%)	Struggling (20%)
Loved and supported	Loved and supported	Relationships with parents strained
Happy	Current problems of moderate intensity	Unhappy
No significant problems	Past problems settling	Most not living at home
Engaged and achieving to best of ability		Problems of very severe intensity

Over half of the young people in this group (11 of 18) were male. Compared to the thriving group, more had been adopted from the care system (78%), although the proportion of young people with low pre-placement risk scores was similar (41%).

The struggling group

There were 13 young people in the struggling group, all of whom were currently experiencing problems of very significant concern. Problems varied, but commonly included angry, oppositional behaviour towards parents, impulsive and risk-taking behaviour, mental health problems, or strain in the parent–child relationship. Many of the young people in this group had spent time living outside the adoptive family (e.g. accommodated, residential school, specialist mental health unit, moving out at age 16), although all of them still received some support from their adoptive parents. These young people had the most difficult backgrounds of those in the study, with three-quarters being adopted from care and only three of the 13 having a low pre-placement risk score. There were more males (nine of 13) in this group than females. Some of the young people in this group had worrying problems from a young age (five of 13), but other young people did not develop problems until early adolescence.

> Eleanor was adopted at one-and-a-half, and was doing fairly well in her early and middle childhood. Around the time she moved to secondary school, she started to show a range of worrying emotions and behaviours and she stopped attending school. Her behaviours were impulsive and dangerous, and she seemed to push away her adoptive parents, whom she used to be very close to. She had spent time in voluntary care as her parents could not keep her safe, although they remained involved and committed. By age 19 she was living back at home; she had been diagnosed with a mental disorder.

Understanding patterns of development

Our analysis of adoptive parents' accounts of their children's development suggests that a number of factors are important in understanding developmental pathways. Factors that emerged as important were as follows.

- **Genetic predispositions** – some young people had developed difficulties that can have a genetic basis, and which were shared by members of their birth family.

- **Pre-birth risks** – some young people had been harmed by exposure to drugs or alcohol in the womb. This harm was not always apparent at the time the children had been placed for adoption.

- **Pre-placement risks** (exposure to poor quality care and/or frequent changes in caregiver) – as we have seen above, children in the thriving group had the fewest pre-placement risks, and those in the struggling group the highest risks.

- **Post-placement risks** – some young people had experienced further adversity in their lives since being adopted. Examples included bereavement, the divorce of adoptive parents, or being bullied.

- **Normal developmental transitions** – moving from primary to secondary school and the onset of puberty seemed particularly stressful times for many adopted young people and could trigger problems.

- **Post-placement protective factors** – the most important factor in understanding improvements over time seemed to be the love, stability and support that had been provided by adoptive parents. However, it is important to remember that many young people continued to have developmental problems in spite of the help of their adoptive parents. In some cases, children had also been helped by support services from outside of the family, for example, through school or therapeutic services; sadly, such services were not always available when needed.

Summary

Overall, about half of the adopted young people were thriving, 29 per cent were surviving with a mixture of positives and negatives, and 20 per cent were struggling with very serious problems. The vast majority of adopted young people remained supported by their adoptive parents and were positive about their relationships with them. Adoption had been successful in providing the young people with a supportive family base, but this did not always overcome all the young person's problems.

The adoptive families: what contact was taking place with birth relatives?

Virtually all of the young people in this study had a plan at the time of placement to have ongoing contact with an adult birth relative. There were four main ways in which young people were (or were not) in touch with their birth relatives at Time 3.

- **No contact**: there were no meetings and information was not exchanged.
- **One-way indirect contact**: information was sent (through the adoption agency) from one party but was not reciprocated by the other.
- **Two-way indirect contact**: information was exchanged between the adoptive family and the birth relatives. This included letters, cards or photographs sent via the adoption agency. It also included emails and use of social networking websites. In the figure below, indirect contact refers to arrangements where the adopted young person and birth relatives did not meet face-to-face.
- **Direct contact**: birth relatives and young people met each other face-to-face. This could be with or without adoption agency supervision and could take place in a range of venues. Often direct contact was accompanied by indirect contact.

By Time 3, of the 65 young people:

- nineteen (29%) were having no contact with anyone in their birth family;
- nine (13%) had no contact with adult birth relatives but were in touch (direct or indirect) with a sibling;
- nineteen (29%) were having only indirect contact with an adult birth relative (one-way or two-way; some may also have had sibling contact);
- eighteen (28%) were having direct contact with an adult birth relative (some of these may also have had indirect or sibling contact).

Contact had fallen off over the years. For the 65 young people, two had lost contact in their pre-school years, eight by middle childhood, and 19 by late adolescence.

Which birth relatives were young people in touch with?

The numbers and percentage of the 65 young people in touch with various birth relatives are given below. These figures only include contact where the young person met or received some information from the birth relative.

Contact with birth relatives

	Number	Percentage	Types of contact
Birth mother	25	38	Some direct and some indirect
Birth father	10	15	Some direct and some indirect
Maternal grandparents	12	18	Usually direct
Paternal grandparents	2	3	All indirect
Aunt/uncle	6	9	All direct
Siblings living with birth relatives	12	18	Usually direct
Adopted or fostered siblings	10	15	Usually direct

- In general, young people were having more contact with mothers and maternal grandparents compared to fathers and paternal grandparents.
- Indirect contact was being used more commonly with birth parents than with extended family members.
- Most contact events took place quite infrequently, usually just once or twice a year.
- However, of the 26 young people in direct contact with a birth relative (adult or sibling), a substantial minority were now having fairly frequent meetings (four young people had contact 3–5 times a year and seven young people had contact 6–10 times a year).

To look at whether contact might be related to overall development, we coded the following four contact variables (n=65).

- Young person had any direct contact with adult birth relatives since placement (n=35, 54%).
- Young person had any contact with adult birth relatives since age 11 (n=44, 68%).
- Young person had been in any form of contact with a birth relative from whose care they had been removed because of concerns about abuse or neglect (a "risky" birth relative) (n= 28, 43%).
- The number of birth relatives the young people had been in contact with in the last 12 months: this ranged from 0 to 11 birth relatives. The mean number was low (1.5) and just eight young people (12%) had been in touch with four or more birth relatives in the last year.

The table below shows young people's contact arrangements (using these four variables) according to their overall "outcome of adoption" group. There are no strong indications that birth family contact was related to the young people's overall adjustment.

Summary

By late adolescence, just over two-thirds of the young people were still in contact with at least one birth relative and more contact was taking place with maternal birth relatives than paternal birth family relatives. Contact had continued to diminish over time, and most ongoing arrangements remained infrequent. However, some young people had recently started to have more frequent contact or contact with a broader range of birth relatives. Contact arrangements did not appear to be related to young people's overall adjustment.

Young people's overall outcomes and contact arrangements

	Have had direct contact	Have had any contact since age 11	Contact with "risky" birth relative	Number of birth relatives in contact with in last 12m
Thriving (n=32)	n=19, 59.4%	n=21, 65.6%	n=13, 40.6%	M=1.8, sd=2.3 Median = 1
Surviving (n=18)	n=9, 50%	n=12, 66.7%	n=6, 33%	M=1.2, sd=1.2 Median = 1
Struggling (n=13)	n=6, 46.2%	n=10, 76.9%	n=7, 53.8%	M=1.5, sd=1.6 Median = 1

Adoptive families' experiences of direct contact

Over time, about half (20 of 39, 51%) of direct contact arrangements were still ongoing. Five arrangements had changed to two-way indirect contact (13%) and 14 arrangements (36%) had stopped altogether. Direct contact was more likely to have lasted over time if it was with a grandparent or sibling as opposed to the birth parent. Only a minority (29%) of direct contact plans with birth parents had lasted. These broad figures just provide a snapshot – there had often been fluctuations over time with some plans having both increases and decreases over the years.

The direct contact arrangements experienced by the families were all voluntary arrangements; adoptive parents could change or stop contact depending on how well it was going. Also, as children became teenagers, some decided to make changes to the contact themselves. So some contact arrangements had reduced because adoptive parents or young people were unhappy with the contact. This was not always the case, however; in particular, some contact arrangements had ceased because the birth relative had died or (less commonly) chosen to withdraw from the contact. Most adoptive parents and young people identified a mixture of benefits and challenges related to having direct contact.

Benefits identified by adoptive parents

- **Enhancing adoptive family relationships**, for example, through creating an atmosphere of openness in the family and sharing important experiences with the young person.
- **Extra support to children and young people**, for example, the child feeling loved and cared about by their birth family and contact helping the child's sense of wholeness or identity.
- **Support to adoptive parents**, for example, gaining a sense of relief that birth relatives would not turn up "out of the blue", getting emotional support from birth relatives when children were experiencing difficulties, finding out information about the birth family.

We had frequent enough contact that she built a relationship and we've got loads of photographs and this sort of thing and she remembers them, so I'd never have forgiven myself if at 12 or 13 I'd have told her 'oh by the way, you're adopted and your parents died'. How would you ever get over that rift with your child? (Adoptive mother; direct contact with birth parents, both now deceased)

I would say the positive is he's grown up with the knowledge that he lives with us because he was loved but his parents were both ill. Unlike some adopted people who feel unloved, I think [birth father] has shown him real affection. (Adoptive mother; direct contact with birth father)

And I suppose for me as well, a mother popping up out of the blue would feel very threatening so I don't have that threat because we already have that relationship with her. (Adoptive mother; direct contact with birth mother)

It's got benefits from the point of view of now we've met his mother and also talking to [maternal grandmother] over the years, it's made us understand Sean's potential weaknesses and strengths genetically. There's no doubt about it, he's got a lot of the way his mother is and it helped us to maybe steer him away from certain situations. (Adoptive mother; direct contact with maternal grandmother)

Benefits identified by young people

- **Help with understanding why they were adopted**, for example, through talking with birth relatives or seeing their birth parents' needs and difficulties.
- **Building identity**, through identifying likenesses to birth relatives, and understanding their genetic heritage.
- **Enjoying close relationships** with birth relatives.

> I don't know if I know everything but I speak to my nan like once a week on the phone and we've had long chats and she's told me everything…Well she (birth mother) is always ringing up my nan, like trying to get out of problems and stuff, and she's really unorganised and stuff, so nan still has to do loads of stuff for her…I see [my grandmother] more as a friend now, like I can talk to her about anything. Like not even bothered if it isn't about my past. Just like talking to her in general really. (Emily, 19; direct contact with maternal grandmother)

> Seeing people who look like me: it's quite nice in a way because, like, my best friend – she really looks like her mum. (Abbie, 17; direct contact with birth mother)

> Some of the information I learned and photos I saw made me feel like I was learning about myself. Where my nose came from, why I enjoy art so much. (Daisy, 20; direct contact with grandparents)

Challenges identified by adoptive parents

- **Practical issues** such as finding a comfortable and safe place to meet.
- **Working out roles and boundaries**, and thinking about how these might change as the young person becomes an adult.
- A reminder that the **child has another family**.
- The **emotional strain** of meetings.

> Even now I would say there's a touch of agitation…I suppose there's two things. One is you're spending time with people that you don't really know all that well. You have this odd link with them that's not based on friendship or family or background or anything…And then there's also…it's just another reminder that she's not 100% yours. So, I have to cope with that…There's always that bit of relief when we get home that it went alright.

A small number of adopters chose to end the contact meetings for various reasons. These tended to be people who reported feeling pressured to agree to direct contact from the outset. They felt that they had been the victims of a 'social work fad' as one person put it, and some had feared that they would not be accepted as adopters if they had not complied. For these people, once they had legally adopted the child, there was little motivation to overcome even fairly minor problems with the contact and they were quick to withdraw.

Sadly, there were two cases where direct contact had been planned for children who had been severely abused or rejected by the contact birth relative. In one case, it was clear that the child was distressed by the contact and it was stopped very early on. In the other case, it continued for several years, with the adoptive parent feeling that the child gained nothing from it.

Challenges identified by young people

The main challenge of direct contact identified by young people was dealing with the emotional strain of meetings, for example, seeing a mentally ill parent, feeling sad for a birth parent, not knowing how to talk to birth relatives, or dealing with the death or serious illness of the birth parent. This element of strain was apparent to some degree in all contact meetings with birth parents but was rarely reported when contact was with grandparents. Nevertheless, most young people were glad that they had had the contact, even though in some cases they had decided not to continue it once they were 18.

> It's helpful in a way because you need to know, say when I am 18 if I do meet up with [my birth mother] on my own, I'm going to need to know that she does have good and bad times, but I think sometimes it can make you think 'Hang on a minute, if she's going to be like that, am I going to be like that?' It can...it gives you something to think about in the back of your mind that you don't really want but you know you need to have there.

> Obviously when you're younger you haven't got all the thoughts there, you just go along thinking you're just meeting up with some people. But when you get older you start thinking more about it. But I wouldn't say it was hard. It's just not very easy. It's not hard but it's just not easy.

Summary

About half of the direct contact arrangements had stopped altogether or changed to indirect contact. This was sometimes because the adoptive parents or young people (or occasionally birth relatives) were unhappy with the contact, but in other cases it was because birth relatives had died. Contact was usually a mixture of benefits and challenges. Contact with grandparents was generally more straightforward, less emotionally strained, and more likely to last than contact with birth parents.

Adoptive families' experiences of indirect contact

Indirect contact arrangements had fallen off over time to an even greater extent than direct contact arrangements. By Time 3, in 64 per cent of indirect contact cases (38 of 59) the adopted young person was not receiving any correspondence from their birth relative.

Most indirect contact arrangements that had faltered had done so relatively early in the placement. Some adoptive parents had withdrawn from contact because they found it emotionally difficult, or because they were unhappy with the nature of a birth parent's reply. More commonly, adoptive parents had withdrawn from contact because they were not receiving a reply from birth relatives; some had concluded that their letters were not wanted, and others felt that letterbox contact was of no value to the young person without a reply.

There were eight families where adoptive parents were sending letters to birth relatives in spite of receiving no reply. In six of these cases, the expectation from the start had been for one-way contact; these parents did not have the same sense of disappointment or being let down as in those cases where a reply from the birth parent was expected. Adoptive parents continued to send a letter because they wanted to honour their original commitment, acknowledge the child's connection to their birth family, and/or out of empathy for the birth family.

> I guess I feel an obligation…not to the agency, it's more to [birth mother] and [adopted child] I suppose really. I sort of think if I was in her shoes I'd like to get them. Just human being to human being. Because fundamentally birth parents aren't bad, who knows what she's doing now, what her difficulties are.

Some indirect contact arrangements (11 of 59, 19%) had developed into face-to-face meetings. Most commonly, this change was at the young person's instigation in adolescence. Some young people wanted to make this change because indirect contact had been positive and they felt ready to meet their birth parent; where this was the case, meetings were usually (although not always) successful.

Others wanted to meet their birth parent because indirect contact had been unsuccessful (for example, birth relatives did not reply) and they had been left with unanswered questions or unmet needs; in such situations, meetings with birth relatives were more mixed.

There were eight families who were still having two-way indirect contact at Time 3; four cases were where one-way contact had become two-way, usually because adoptive parents had requested a reply from birth relatives. In the other four families, two-way indirect contact had been sustained from the start. Where two-way exchanges of letters had taken place, adoptive parents and young people identified a very similar range of benefits, including:

- **keeping the birth family "alive"** in the adoptive family;
- reducing the young person's **sense of rejection**;
- **answering specific questions** raised by the young person;
- **getting information** about other birth relatives, such as siblings who were born after the adoption;
- **preparing the young person** for the possibility of a future meeting.

Benefits of two-way indirect contact: case example

Lily's birth mother relinquished her as a baby. Lily's adoptive parents met with her birth mother and an annual exchange of letters and photographs was planned. This arrangement endured and all parties found it helpful and positive. As Lily got older, she became involved in deciding what should be sent and occasionally asked her adoptive mother to request specific information, which her birth mother always provided. From her mid-teens, Lily was determined to meet her birth mother and she did this, with her adoptive mother, when she was 18 years old. This reunion has proved positive for all concerned. Lily and her adoptive mother felt that the indirect contact had helped them to feel familiar with the birth mother and her subsequent family over the years, and this was highly beneficial when it came to the reunion.

Challenges of indirect contact reported by adoptive parents

- **Dealing with birth parents** who did not respond.

- **Knowing what to say in letters**, for example, whether to mention things like holidays or life advantages that the birth relatives might not have, dealing with the feelings of teenagers who might not want information shared.

- **Not knowing if or when to end the contact** once the young person became an adult.

Challenges of indirect contact reported by young people

- **Feeling hurt** when birth parents wrote about caring for their pets or other children.

- **A sense of distance** or strangeness because they did not know the people sending the letters.

- **Feeling hurt and rejected** because the birth relative had failed to respond.

- **Finding writing or receiving letters emotional**.

Challenges of two-way indirect contact: case example

Toby was placed for adoption when he was four months old. His adoptive parents met his birth mother and agreed an annual indirect exchange of letters and photographs. Toby's birth mother responded once or twice and then stopped. When Toby was about seven years old, he said that he did not want his adoptive parents to send information about him to his birth mother as it made him feel "different". The adoptive parents felt that the contact did not benefit Toby in any way and did not send any further information.

Summary

Where two-way indirect contact was sustained over time, it had a range of benefits for adoptive parents and adopted young people. However, the majority of indirect contact arrangements (which were almost always with birth parents) had been problematic over the years, and the complexity of trying to communicate through the written word, and where little is known about the person you are writing to, was apparent. A lack of replies from birth parents was a common problem, and where replies were expected but not received, adoptive parents and young people often felt let down and disappointed.

The satisfaction of young people with their contact arrangements

Interview data were used to code young people's contact satisfaction, as follows.

- **High satisfaction** (n=17, 53%): Although these young people may have experienced some challenges with contact, they highlighted more benefits and were happy overall with the contact they had experienced.

- **Moderate/mixed satisfaction** (n=10, 31%): These young people experienced benefits and challenges from contact in roughly equal measure, and would have liked to have changed some aspects of their contact.

- **Low satisfaction** (n= 5, 16%): These young people experienced more challenges than benefits from contact and they would have preferred a different type of contact.

Contact satisfaction was coded in relation to how the young people felt contact had worked out overall over the course of their childhood. Where contact had resulted in a recent reunion with birth relatives, it was the satisfaction with the contact that was experienced before the reunion that was coded.

High satisfaction

- Five young people had experienced regular direct contact with an adult birth relative;
- Six had very minimal contact, usually one-way contact to their birth parents.
- Six had ongoing two-way indirect contact; four had now met their birth parent/s.

Almost all the young people in this group had experienced relatively stable contact arrangements from the start of their placement. Their contact arrangements were familiar to them, and to them seemed normal, hence the stability of contact contributed to satisfaction. These contact arrangements had also remained stable because the adoptive families were happy with the arrangement.

I like to see that he's OK and that he's safe…I think it's better to see them, even if they're not OK…I think it is good…I don't think there is any way that it could be done better. (Henry, aged 20, face-to-face contact with birth father)

If you could wave a magic wand, would you change anything about contact?

No, not really. I think that, well, I think having one or two letters and photos here is better than not having any contact but I think too much contact would be…that would make it worse…I think that the contact I've had is enough…It's not too little but it's not lots of contact. (Blake, aged 17, two-way indirect contact with birth father)

At the moment I'm living a very happy life here…I wouldn't change anything about the contact because I think it's just been right. We've sent the letters, we have the photos and I feel that's just about enough. Again, when I'm older, maybe meeting up would be very nice because I'd rather have the face-to-face to sustain that relationship perhaps for life, to have that image in my head…So I think I'd keep the contact the same. (Justin, aged 18, one-way contact with birth parents)

My dad abused someone ten years before I was born so I'm, like, I don't really want to meet him, and my mum's a drug addict now, so I don't want to meet her either.

And how do you feel about not having had any contact with them?

I'm fine with it. (Ashley, aged 14, no contact)

Moderate satisfaction

Some young people in this group highlighted both advantages and disadvantages of the contact that they had experienced. Other young people were happy with contact arrangements with one birth relative, but were unhappy about their contact with others. Again, the contact experienced had been diverse, but few arrangements had been stable over time. The instability of contact caused dissatisfaction in young people, but also at times reflected their dissatisfaction, for example, if they were finding contact difficult they might seek a temporary break from it.

- One young person had never had any contact.
- One young person was unaware of the indirect contact with his birth mother until he was a teenager; he then became involved in this contact.
- One young person had two-way indirect contact that had been erratic and which then stopped.
- Seven young people had experienced both direct and indirect contact arrangements. These had fluctuated over the years, and in some cases had stopped completely.

If I could get my mum to write to me I would do that. And my dad as well. Not so much my aunt because I didn't really live with her, but my mum and dad and brother, because he was, like, part of me. (Rosie, aged 14, had direct contact with brother, and letters from mother. Was sad, disappointed and confused about these contacts stopping.)

It's good to know I was being thought of but at the same time I still feel like they [grandparents] think they know me and I don't feel like I know them. I felt a lot of pressure when meeting them, as I do with meeting new people. I do want a relationship with my grandparents, I'm just not sure how to build one or even why I want one.

Is there anything you'd like to be different about the contact?

Maybe get all the awkward "getting to know each other" stuff out of the way. (Daisy, aged 20, had letters from and visits with grandparents; meetings had stopped and started as Daisy's feelings about them fluctuated)

I just want to see him. I want to see him, I want to meet him, and if he's a horrible person then I'll deal with that then. I'd rather think positive about him because he hasn't done nothing wrong yet, not personally that I've experienced…

If I could wave a magic wand and change anything about your contact, what would you change?

I'd say to have contact with birth dad. (Kiera, aged 17, had positive direct contact with birth mother and grandmother but was very unhappy at having no contact with birth father)

Low satisfaction

Again, contact arrangements were diverse.

- One young person had direct contact with extended family members, and indirect contact with his birth mother; he decided to stop this contact.
- Four people had indirect contact with birth relatives; one of these had never received a reply. Three of these young people had instigated a meeting with one or both of their birth parents in late adolescence.

Why did you decide to stop [contact]?

Because at the time it was like, very, I was very emotional and things like that so I just wanted to focus on one family rather than two. And it was difficult enough with this family, let alone other things…It's easier

to focus on life rather than having to, like, I don't know, it's weird. (James, aged 17, found contact too difficult in the context of all his other problems in life)

....

I guess looking back on it I probably, I think contact now, like if I was ever to adopt, I wouldn't like to adopt someone knowing that they'd have any kind of contact, just because I think that...you're up and you're down. You put this person on a pedestal and then, like, they're never going to exceed what you think they're going to be like. (Marianne, aged 19, had indirect contact with her birth mother, then met her aged 16. Was unhappy because she felt that the indirect contact had given her an unrealistic impression of her birth mother)

....

I wanted to know why I couldn't see her, that's been The Question. There are things that stem off that and spiral into different things like, 'What if she doesn't like me?' but the main question is 'Why can't I see her and why was I adopted and where do they live?' Even in Year 11 I used to trawl through Facebook because I found out her name. (Rees, aged 20, was unhappy that he had so little contact with his birth mother)

....

I think that's kind of damaged me as in I don't like leaving people now...Where you've been moved around a lot during your life you grow bonds with each person and then you get torn away from each one...With my birth mum I would have liked contact but maybe in, like, those contact centre things where you have someone present to make sure there's nothing wrong and stuff...So we could meet up and have the conversations that we needed to have, so we could get everything out in the open. (Graham had letterbox contact with his birth mother and met her again in his 20s. He felt it would have been helpful for face-to-face contact not to have been stopped.)

Factors associated with contact satisfaction

- The type of contact young people had experienced did not seem related to satisfaction, but stability of contact arrangements was associated with higher satisfaction, and erratic contact arrangements with lower satisfaction.

- The fit between the young person's felt need and the extent to which their openness arrangements met that need was important. So while some young people were happy with little or no contact, for others this was a big problem.

- The quality of contact was relevant. In particular, it seems important that contact could help young people achieve a realistic picture of their birth family (avoiding both idealisation and demonisation), answer the young person's questions, and help the young person to deal with feelings of loss or rejection.

- The young person's overall adjustment seemed associated with their satisfaction with contact – young people who were satisfied with their contact tended to be better adjusted overall. This could be because some had more resources to cope with the emotional complexity of contact compared to others. But in some cases, young people linked their poor adjustment to their unhappiness with contact. Common factors may underpin both overall adjustment and satisfaction with contact, for example, a history of abuse and neglect.

Summary

Approximately half of young people were very happy with their contact arrangements; the remainder had mixed feelings or were very unhappy. The type of contact experienced did not appear related to satisfaction. Young people tended to be more satisfied with their contact when it had been stable over time, when it fitted with their felt needs, when it was of good quality, and when their life was generally going well.

The adoptive families: adoption communication openness

The adoption communication openness (ACO) of adoptive parents (in most cases the adoptive mother) was rated from interviews (n=42). Five dimensions were explored, and parents were rated from one (low) to five (high) on each dimension:

- communication with the young person about adoption;
- comfort with and promotion of dual connection;
- empathy with the young person's feelings about adoption;
- empathy with the birth family;
- communication with the birth family.

Adoptive parents in the study were generally rated fairly highly.

Where ACO scores were high, the majority of parents had experienced direct contact arrangements. As we noted at Time 2, contact arrangements and ACO seemed to be linked as communicatively open parents promoted higher levels of contact.

> I couldn't love them any more if they were birth children, but they have got a background that I don't belong to and I'm not part of. And that won't change. And that won't change for any adopted child, ever. They've got a past that belongs away from the adoptive family…I think that they should have that other side because it gives them a feeling of self-worth, it makes them whole.

In other families, aspects of parents' ACO, such as their comfort with dual connection, meant that parents felt less willing to have much contact.

> From our point of view he's ours and we weren't that willing to be too flexible about sharing. We would never have entertained a meeting. We wouldn't have met them because we do feel adoption is, it's a legal cut-off point and…that would be cruel, to encourage them to hang on to him.

Having birth family contact could also promote family communication about adoption.

> I should think after every contact we do have a little bit of a conversation about something to do with adoption or contact or birth families, and how she's feeling about that and how I'm feeling about that…that's a lot more open now so that's a good thing to be able to open up.

In most cases, adoptive parents' ACO scores at Time 2 and Time 3 were very similar, indicating that parents had been consistent in their feelings and behaviour over time. Adoptive parents had experienced new challenges in relation to ACO as their children became teenagers; some young people took a great interest in talking and thinking about adoption, while others shifted their focus elsewhere.

> He's a normal 22-year-old, he's got lots going on outside, his mind is all around girls and enjoying himself. But if you was to sit down and say to him, 'Have you given any thought about your nan lately?', then he'd say, 'Oh, how is she, I'm worried about her,' or something like that. She clearly loves him and I think there's love and affection in return from him. So I think it's something we would encourage.

When young people were uninterested in their adoption or resistant to discussion, adoptive parents with high ACO worked to keep the possibility of a dialogue open in a non-confrontational way.

Others felt that it was best to restrict communication, especially if their child was having problems.

> We hardly ever talk about adoption now... there is no need to keep rehashing it because she doesn't want to bring it up. When she does bring it up we answer everything as truthfully as we know...Otherwise it's playing on their minds the whole time and these are young, vulnerable kids that don't need to keep raking through the past.

Where direct contact had been sustained, adoptive parents had come to know birth relatives as people, with strengths as well as weaknesses. It was easier for adoptive parents to develop empathy where birth relatives were supportive of the adoption.

> It's had nothing but a positive effect, contact. [Grandmother]'s treated us well, this is where I've got a lot of time for her...We've got a lot of empathy for her, she's the one who put him into care, she made a massive decision there because she thought she couldn't look after him so we've got nothing but respect for her.

Where empathy for birth relatives was restricted, it was usually in situations where there was little or no contact with them.

Summary

Most adoptive parents were communicatively open, with over half scoring in the high range. Adoptive parents who scored highest on ACO were more likely to have children who were engaging in direct contact with birth relatives. This seems to be because these parents had chosen more open arrangements, and also because the direct contact had promoted adoption communication openness.

Adoption communication openness (ACO) of adoptive parents and their experiences of contact

ACO scores	Direct contact	No direct contact
High (21 to 25)	n=15 60%	n=7 41.2%
Moderate (15 to 20)	n=7 28%	n=5 29.4%
Low (5 to 14)	n=3 12%	n=5 29.4%
Totals	n=25 100%	n=17 100%

Young people's perspectives on adoption communication openness

Young people completed Brodzinsky's questionnaire about their views of the adoption communication openness of their parents, as well as their own comfort in discussing adoption. Thirty-three young people completed this about their mother, and 30 about their father. Results were as follows:

- Seventy-eight per cent of young people's scores about their mother were very high.
- Sixty-seven per cent of young people's scores about their father were very high.
- Scores for mothers and fathers were significantly related.

We also asked in the interview about young people's experiences of talking about adoption with their parents. They were asked to select from a list of things or people that had helped them to understand the reasons for their adoption. Nearly all (28 of 31) selected their adoptive mother, and 18 of 31 selected their adoptive father. Thus, overall it seemed that most young people were happy with the way their parents approached talking about adoption, and that generally more of this communication was taking place with mothers compared to fathers.

Many young people reported being told about adoption from a very young age.

> **Mum and Dad must have told me since I was little because I can't remember a specific day or point, and you'd remember, wouldn't you? I've always known that I was adopted.**

Most young people did not worry that their parents would be upset if they asked questions.

> **They've always been really open about it, we don't have to be scared of 'Can we talk about our birth family in front of them, will they get upset?' because they've been there from the beginning and always said it's fine to talk about it.**

A few young people did not feel that their parents were open with them.

> **When I ask [adoptive mother] about it, she always seems to sort of put it off. Not put it off but be, like, 'I'll go through it with you someday' but, like, that day never comes...I suppose, like, now I'm getting older I want to know more of who I am. I've got no one really to ask who knows...I don't think she finds it hard, but I just always think that she's, like, hiding something, well, not hiding something but there's still a lot more to know that she hasn't told me. I don't ask that much, I just sort of accept it.**

Young people who had made contact with birth relatives in their later teens or been through reunion meetings had mostly done this with their adoptive mother beside them, and mothers were often key in helping them to process their feelings at these times.

> **We wrote her [birth mother], me and my mum we wrote her a message on Facebook and it went from there really.**

Summary

Most young people in the study were happy with the communication they had with their adoptive parents about adoption. There were some indications that young people talked more about adoption with their mothers than with their fathers.

Being adopted: young people's construction of an adoptive identity

From a qualitative analysis of the interviews with 32 young people, we identified four different patterns of identity formation: cohesive, unexplored, developing, and fragmented. Details of the young people in each of these groups are given in the table below.

Cohesive adoptive identity: key themes

- High levels of exploration about adoption.
- Detailed and coherent stories that seemed realistic.
- Thoughtful about their own feelings and the perspectives of others.
- Were "at ease" with their adoption story, even if this was difficult.
- Emotional responses were appropriate, but difficult feelings were not overwhelming.
- Strong sense of connection to their adoptive family.
- Saw the reason for their adoption as understandable, necessary or justified.
- Views of birth family varied from case to case.

> All that I really know is that when my birth mum was born, her mum didn't have a very good upbringing so didn't really know how to look after her. She kept her but she didn't really know what she was doing. So when it came to my birth mum having kids, because she hadn't been brought up brilliant by her mum she didn't know how to bring us up, because she didn't have a big enough mother figure. I think when she was younger she mixed a lot with the wrong people and with drugs and everything and with not knowing what she was doing. Either her or social services thought it was safer for us to be adopted because not only was she doing the drugs but the little that she did know wasn't much because she hadn't been given it by her own mum.

Unexplored adoptive identity: key themes

- Very low levels of exploration of adoption: gave very simple accounts of why they were adopted.
- "At ease" with their adoption stories; their story made sense to them.
- Saw adoption entirely as a positive experience.
- Unquestioning acceptance of adoptive parents.
- Views of birth relatives were unquestioning – could be positive (when birth relatives were known) or uninterested (when they were not known).

Patterns of identity formation

Identity group	Number	Age range	Mean age	Male	Female
Cohesive	16	14–22	18y10m	5	11
Unexplored	5	15–21	17y10m	5	0
Developing	5	14–21	18y10m	2	3
Fragmented	6	17–20	18y8m	4	2

- Four of the five young people had learning difficulties; these may have limited exploration.

....

I just know that she couldn't look after me, that's about it.

And any idea why she couldn't look after you?

I don't know really.

....

It doesn't bother me about my other parents, my birth parents.

Developing adoptive identity: key themes

- Questions about adoption not fully resolved – unanswered questions, partial explanations and feelings of being uninformed were common.
- Uncertain, unsettled or contradictory feelings about the birth family.
- Feelings of wanting and needing to find out more.
- Adoptive family clearly seen as "my family".

....

I mean over the years, but even more recently I keep wanting to ask 'How did my dad die?' or so many things like that, or 'Am I able to get in contact with my birth mum?' or 'How would I go about doing that?' I do tend to ask these questions again and again because I just like to reminisce on those thoughts.

....

I think I've basically always known the story, but, like, I want to know more because I don't feel I know enough. I think I know only the basic gist of it.

So can you put your finger on the sort of things that you'd like to know that you feel you don't know?

Yeah, sort of more about [my birth parents]. So, like, who they were and if I have anything in common with them. To find out like who I am, sort of thing.

Fragmented adoptive identity: key themes

- Narratives about adoption lacked coherence and were often rigid, "stuck" or seemed to be "going round in circles".
- Some young people avoided exploration of adoption because they were very anxious about what they might find.
- Strong presence of negative feelings such as anger, sadness or loss – at life in general, or specifically about adoption.
- Four young people felt a connection with their adoptive parents, but two had a shaky sense of belonging in their adoptive family.
- Ambivalent feelings about their birth family.
- Feeling that being adopted was a source of stigma or emotional turbulence.

....

I have no idea [why I was adopted], it could be completely different. That's the story that I've been told, but I have no idea. It's that uncertainty which hurts...I don't know if you sort of fully understand the degree that it bothers me...And it can bother me daily, even now...It's like a burn.

....

Do you talk to any of your other friends about [adoption]?

No. Because I'm frightened they'll take the piss, basically. I've told one person who's my friend and he's sort of, 'I bet that's gutting for you'.

How did overall development, communication about adoption, and contact arrangements relate to identity development?

- **Overall development**: almost all young people in the cohesive, unexplored and developing identity groups were thriving in their development overall. In contrast, none of the young people with a fragmented adoptive identity were thriving. Their problems in life may have affected their capacity to cope with adoption-related stress. For three of these six young people, adoption issues were dominant in their life and added to their overall problems.

- **Adoption communication openness**: the adoption communication openness (ACO) of adoptive parents varied within each identity group. Differences between groups were not stark; our sample was small and most adoptive parents in the study scored quite highly. Using researcher ratings of ACO, scores were highest for parents whose children were in the cohesive group (mean = 22) and developing group (mean = 21), and were lower in the unexplored (mean = 19) and fragmented groups (mean = 18). Results were similar when using adopted young people's ratings of ACO. For example, 87 per cent of young people in the cohesive group rated their mother in the high range versus 66 per cent in the fragmented group.

- **Birth family contact**: across the four identity groups, a wide range of contact experiences over time was evident. However, there were striking differences between young people in terms of whether or not they had been in touch with birth family members in the last year, with young people in the cohesive identity group having the most contact and those in the fragmented group the least contact. This variable probably most accurately reflects the success of contact over time, as young people had chosen to remain in contact with birth relatives.

Summary

Young people's interest in and feelings about adoption were varied, although few young people were completely uninterested. Four patterns of identity development were identified: cohesive, unexplored, developing, and fragmented. There were some suggestions that both birth family contact and adoptive parent ACO were related to identity development, as contact and communication about adoption provided opportunities for young people to process their thoughts and feelings.

Young people's identity development and their contact arrangements

Identity group	Number	Percentage ever had direct contact	Percentage had any contact since 11	Mean no. of relatives in touch within last year	Percentage in touch with no one in last year
Cohesive	16	(10 of 16) 62.5	(13 of 16) 81	2.4	(3 of 16) 19
Unexplored	5	(2 of 5) 40	(2 of 5) 40	1.2	(3 of 5) 60
Developing	5	(5 of 5) 100	(5 of 5) 100	0.4	(3 of 4) 60
Fragmented	6	(3 of 6) 50	(5 of 6) 83	0.83	(3 of 6) 50

Birth relatives: well-being and adjustment to the adoption, 16 years on

Mental well-being

Twenty-four of the 37 birth relatives (14 parents, 10 extended birth family members) filled in the Brief Symptom Inventory, a measure looking at their mental distress in the last seven days. This showed that 46 per cent of the birth relatives (11 of 24) had levels of mental distress at a clinically significant level. This is much higher than in general community samples. Levels of mental distress were elevated for extended family members (4 of 10) as well as for birth parents (7 of 14). Many birth relatives reported a long history of experiencing mental distress that often predated the child's adoption. Unsurprisingly, however, some birth relatives felt that the adoption had caused feelings of mental distress, and continued to do so in the present day.

Acceptance of the adoption

Using a coding system devised at Time 2 of the study, we coded birth relatives according to their acceptance of the adoption. Three patterns were identified:

- positive acceptance;
- resignation; and
- anger and resistance.

Positive acceptance

- Accepted and supported the child's membership of the adoptive family.
- Expressed positive feelings about the child's life in their adoptive family.
- Realistic about their current and future role in the child's life.
- Saw adoption as having worked out for the best.

Positive acceptance: case example

James had split up with Nicole's mother before she was born. Nicole was taken into care when she was only a few months old. James did not feel able to offer her a home himself as he had no adequate housing, and did not feel capable of looking after a baby. He felt that adoption was a better option for Nicole than staying with her birth mother, but losing Nicole to adoption still made him feel very depressed. James exchanged letters with the adoptive parents for several years and, when she was older, Nicole also wrote to him. James was delighted to receive the letters, especially from Nicole. He felt very reassured that Nicole was having a good life in her adoptive family, and he felt content that he'd made the right decision. In the last couple of years Nicole had stopped writing to James, but he accepted that she was old enough to decide for herself, and he remained hopeful that the contact might resume in the future.

Resignation

- Felt very unhappy about the adoption, but resigned themselves to the loss.
- Feelings of worthlessness and helplessness in relation to the child.
- Feelings of guilt and anxiety about the child.
- A passive approach.

Resignation: case example

Carla has three children, all of whom were taken into care and adopted. Carla has learning difficulties, she had a difficult upbringing herself, and she struggles to manage in her day-to-day life. She recognised that the home environment provided for her children was not good enough; she did not resist them being taken away and adopted because she felt resistance would not make any difference. Her feelings of loss about her children had not diminished over the years; she said she thought about them 'a lot' and this made her feel 'sad, upset'. When her children were younger she had received some minimal contact in the form of letters from the adoptive parents. However, this had stopped without any explanation. Carla was upset and angry about this, but had not taken any action to find out why. She hoped that she might see her children again one day, but was worried that she wouldn't be able to answer their questions.

Anger and resistance

- Whilst not necessarily actively opposing the adoption, it is not accepted in the birth relative's heart.
- Dismissive of the child's relationship with the adoptive parents; sees self as the "real" parent.
- High levels of anger directed externally, for example, towards social workers, courts, family, adoptive parents.

Anger and resistance: case example

Harold was angry with both social services and his former wife that his daughter had been adopted. He felt that it should never have happened and that she belonged with him, as he could have given her a good life. He was dismissive of any opportunities that adoption might have offered her and felt that he could have provided the things that really matter. He thought he would try to trace his daughter through social networking websites, although he acknowledged that he should wait until she was 18 before doing this. He hoped that he would be reunited with her one day, but stated that he would not wish to meet her adoptive parents.

At Time 3, just over two-thirds of the birth relatives were rated as having positive acceptance (68%, 25); just over a quarter were resigned (27%, 10); and two were angry and resistant (5%, 2).

As was the case at Time 2, extended family members were more likely than birth parents to be in the positive acceptance group. Ninety per cent (18 of 20) of extended birth family members positively accepted the adoption, whereas only 41 per cent (7 of 17) of birth parents positively accepted the adoption. The two remaining extended birth family members were in the resigned group. Of the remaining birth parents, eight were resigned and two were angry and resistant to the adoption at Time 3.

Of the 31 birth relatives whose interview data were coded at both stages, 26 (84%) remained in the same acceptance category. Three birth relatives had moved from feeling resigned to positively accepting the adoption at Time 3. Two birth relatives had moved from positively accepting the adoption to feeling resigned at Time 3. Where birth relatives felt more accepting of the adoption over time, this was associated with positive experiences of contact, and the young person progressing well. Where birth relatives felt less accepting over time, this was associated in one case with contact ceasing with no explanation, and in the other case with the young person becoming very disturbed as a teenager, leaving the birth parent feeling increasingly guilty about the child's care in earlier life.

Challenges for birth relatives in the young people's teenage years

Some birth relatives had faced new issues as the young people became teenagers.

- Where young people developed problems in adolescence, some birth relatives reflected on their own role in causing these problems.
- Feelings that the adoption had "been for the best" could be challenged where young people were having lots of problems.

- Where young people were having problems, birth relatives needed to think about their role in helping the young person; this was especially so where the young person was not getting on with their adoptive parents.

- Birth relatives thought increasingly about what might happen to the contact arrangements once the child became an adult. Many birth relatives who were not in direct contact with the young person were thinking about the possibility of the young person wanting to meet them, sometimes in hope, but sometimes with anxiety.

- Some birth relatives had experienced contact ceasing when the young person was a teenager, often without much explanation.

....

I must prepare myself because he might ask questions like, 'Why did you have me adopted?' He might feel a bit hurtful because I've got the kids here and he'll think 'Why was I the only one adopted?'...and I'll have to explain that to him. (Resigned birth mother, indirect contact)

....

I think you bear it in mind that if you keep it up that you're going to see them one day. Of course, it is a loss but you just think they're a long way away and you wouldn't see them anyway.

And how do you feel about the possibility of that meeting?

Blooming overjoyed. It would be nice, even if it was just once a year. (Positively accepting grandparent, indirect contact)

....

I know he has a lot of trouble with his adoptive mum and dad and I know they don't see eye to eye. I obviously only hear his side so I don't see what's going on, I don't know if he's just being a rebel, growing up as they do, or...I don't know...I've not agreed with some of the things they've done or the actions they've taken but I've never told him that. They're the ones bringing him up, I can't start interfering. (Positively accepting grandparent, face-to-face contact)

....

I feel guilty because I think it's my fault... Because I should have been there for her when she was little instead of being into me drinking and bad blokes, I should have looked after her more. (Resigned birth mother, face-to-face contact)

Summary

Almost half of the birth relatives had high levels of psychological distress 16 years after the adoption. Two-thirds were able to positively accept the adoption; extended family members were more likely to be in this group than birth parents. Birth relatives had faced additional challenges in managing their feelings about adoption during the young person's teenage years. These were linked to managing feelings about the young person's developmental difficulties, and to anticipating changes in contact as the young person approached adulthood.

The birth relatives: contact pathways and experiences

We looked at the main type of contact that birth relatives were having with the adopted young person at Time 3. Where birth relatives had contact with more than one adopted child, we used the child with whom they had the most contact to code the "main" type of contact. In order to avoid double counting, where we had interviewed two birth relatives about the same contact (for example, husband and wife), we counted this contact once – hence the figures below are based on 30 cases.

- Overall, 60 per cent (18 of 30) of cases were still in touch with at least one adopted young person.

- Twelve birth relatives (40%; seven birth parents and five extended birth family members) were not having any contact with any of their children.

- Eleven birth relatives (36.6%) were having some form of indirect contact: of these, seven (two birth parents and five extended family members) were having two-way indirect contact, two birth parents were just receiving (and not reciprocating) information from the adoptive family, and the same number (two birth parents) were just sending information (and not receiving anything in return).

- Seven birth relatives (23%) were having direct contact – this included three birth parents and four extended family members.

Where contact was still happening, for all but two birth relatives the frequency was between one–three times a year. However, there were two birth relatives in the sample who were now in very frequent contact with the adopted young person; a grandparent who had kept up direct contact over time, which had increased in the teenage years, and a birth mother who had kept up indirect contact and then developed a face-to-face relationship with her child as a young adult.

In 11 of the 12 cases where birth relatives were no longer having contact, contact had ceased between Time 2 and Time 3.

Benefits of direct contact experienced by birth relatives

Birth relatives who had sustained direct contact over time were very positive about their experiences. The key benefits identified by the relatives were:

- knowing that the child was well and happy;
- easing feelings of guilt and loss; and
- developing a relationship with the young person.

> Yeah, I wasn't sure at first whether I wanted to carry on seeing her because I thought it would be really difficult, but it was just nice to see her grow up and have the life that she's got now, which I could never have given her, not at that time anyway. And she's a wonderful young lady, she really is. She's just passed her driving test. I would never be able to give her what she had then. (Birth mother)

> I did feel that it would have been great if I could have taken him on and I went down to the hospital when he was born. It was a rather strange day because [birth mother] had left him there in intensive care and I saw him there and it was a very great wrench for me not to be able to take him on myself. So the way it worked out with [adoptive mother] has been very good for me personally because I see that he's had so much love from her, this openness has been just enormously valuable. (Grandfather)

Challenges of direct contact experienced by birth relatives

Birth relatives reported very few negatives about having direct contact, although as discussed in the previous section, where young people had developmental problems in adolescence, this could bring about challenges.

One issue that had arisen in several cases was that of protecting the confidentiality of the adoptive family; this was a key issue that several grandparents had to manage if and when the birth parents of the child asked them for identifying information.

Benefits of sustained two-way indirect contact experienced by birth relatives

Where two-way indirect contact was sustained through to the child's late teens, exchanges of information and/or photographs were usually of great significance to birth relatives. Benefits experienced included:

- reassurance about how the child was getting on;
- laying a foundation for future meetings;
- hoping that contact would reduce the child's sense of rejection; and
- seeing likenesses in the child.

> **I think it [indirect contact] is good, just knowing that Ewan is out there and he's doing alright…If I didn't have that link I would probably be thinking, 'Has he died? Has he emigrated?' I'd have been wondering, but I don't have to wonder. (Grandparent)**

> **I didn't feel like I'd lost her completely…I wonder whether if I hadn't had any of that when we met again it would have been a very emotional reunion, but having that contact is very soothing and reassuring. (Birth mother)**

> **I'm sure it sort of helps them to know the other side, the birth family, and that they'll know that, they know that they're important. (Grandparent)**

Challenges of sustained two-way indirect contact experienced by birth relatives

There were some specific difficulties associated with indirect contact. Some of these had been present from the outset; others developed with the passing of time.

- Knowing what information to send or leave out, for example, what to say about other birth family members.
- Receiving worrying information about the child.
- Concern that letters from the adoptive parents did not tell the whole story.
- Understanding how their role could change if and when reunions occurred.

> **I haven't written much about me personally because I haven't had much good going on. (Birth mother)**

> **So there was never any difficulties…only ever glowing praise for her. Which was nice to hear but maybe…I suppose you don't really know, they're still very superficial aren't they, the letters. Very surface level stuff. (Grandparent)**

> **What role do you think you have in her life?**
>
> I don't know. I think that's the funny thing, I really don't, I'm not sure…I'm quite clear that I'm not her mother…she's got a mother…I am very committed to her. It's not an auntie role either. It's not a…I can only describe it as…oh, I don't know what to describe it as [laughs]. I don't know. (Birth mother, met daughter aged 18)

Indirect contact that was not sustained

As noted above, several birth relatives had experienced their indirect contact letters stopping since Time 2. In several cases this had happened with little or no explanation, and this caused particular distress to birth relatives. Birth relatives commonly worried about what had happened to the child; in some cases they were concerned that they might have said or done something to cause the adoptive parents to withdraw from contact. It also left birth relatives wondering what might happen when the child reached the age of 18.

> I just wonder as time went on whether he was becoming more difficult or he…I know he did have to go to a special school in the end and that was the last update that I had from her. Maybe when that happened things became more difficult. It's been really hard having [letter contact] and then breaking it. I would have preferred it to be not at all or obviously carried on. But to have those updates and then just take it away was more difficult I think. (Birth mother)

> I started writing letters 'How's Ella getting on, hope she's doing alright at college and perhaps I could see her some time?' Then I put down that I'd met someone and got another little girl [step-daughter]. I wonder if saying that, they thought 'Oh, he don't want to know about Ella anymore'. (Birth father)

> I keep thinking he's going to come and knock on the door. I'm really starting to get a bit twitchy about that. It's really, really scary, because, like I say, I don't know what [adoptive mother] has told him. Even though she broke contact, I don't know whether she still told him about me. (Birth mother)

Contact satisfaction of birth relatives related to type of contact

Time 3 contact	High satisfaction	Mixed satisfaction	Total
No contact	0	15 (100%)	15
Just sending (one-way BR to AP/YP)	1 (50%)	1 (50%)	2
Just receiving (one-way AP to BR)	1 (33.3%)	2 (66.7%)	3
Two-way indirect	4 (50%)	4 (50%)	8
Direct	7 (77.8%)	2 (22.2%)	9
Total	13	24	37

Birth relatives' satisfaction with contact

Birth relatives' satisfaction with contact was coded from the interviews. About one-third of birth relatives (13 of 37, 35%) had very high satisfaction with their contact – this group comprised largely people who had experienced stable direct or indirect contact arrangements that were still ongoing. About two-thirds of birth relatives had mixed satisfaction with contact – these were people who expressed satisfaction with any form of contact they had been able to have, or were still having, but they were unhappy about arrangements where contact had diminished or ceased. There were no birth relatives who were very unsatisfied with contact; all were grateful and pleased to have had some contact, as opposed to none.

Summary

About 40 per cent of birth relatives had lost contact with the adopted young person, with many arrangements stopping during the adolescent years, often with no explanation. Birth relatives valued contact particularly because of the information it gave them about the adopted child. While birth relatives were largely very satisfied with direct contact, indirect contact appeared to have more challenges in terms of knowing what to write, understanding their role, and coping when contact stopped. Birth relatives' satisfaction with contact seemed strongly linked to whether or not it had continued over time.

Social networking websites: new challenges for adoptive parents, birth relatives and adopted young people

We wanted to learn about whether and how adoptive and birth families might have used social networking websites to find out about or get in touch with each other. We included questions about this in the adoptive parent interview. In our interviews with adopted young people and birth relatives, we did not specifically mention the use of social networking websites (through concern of the ethics of doing so, in case our question prompted people to take action), although we did ask adopted young people and birth relatives if there were any other ways in which they had been in touch. Across the three groups of interviewees (adoptive parents, birth relatives and adopted young people), we found examples of three different ways in which people had used social networking websites:

- information;
- communication; and
- reunification.

Information

Some people (across the groups) who had no or little contact were using social networking websites to find out more information about the other party, such as what they looked like, where they were, etc. They did not plan to make contact with the other party in that way at the time of interview. Five young people and/or adoptive parents were using social networking websites in this way and two birth relatives had downloaded photographs after the adoptive parents had stopped sending them through the letterbox system.

Communication

The largest group of people were those using social networking websites as an active way of keeping in contact with each other. This was most often a natural and easy communication. Nine young people were doing this, mostly with siblings, but two young people used it with birth parents and grandparents. Five birth relatives were keeping in touch with their birth children and/or the latter's adoptive parents in this way.

Reunification

Seven young people had used social networking websites to actively search for birth relatives with whom they had previously had no, or indirect, contact and to make contact with them. Two birth parents were planning to use social networking websites to search for and contact their child once they reached 18, and one had done so but had not received a response.

Positive experiences of using social media

Using social media appeared to be beneficial in the context of established relationships between the adoptive families and birth relatives, for example, to supplement face-to-face contact (especially between the adopted young person and their birth siblings, cousins or grandparents) and in cases where adopted young people had the support of their adoptive parents. The involvement and support of adoptive parents helped young people to manage any difficult situations that arose. Some adoptive parents took an active approach to monitoring and supporting their child's use of social media. The support of adoptive parents was particularly vital where young people sought a reunion with their birth parent. Not all reunions worked out well, but young people generally felt that they had met an important need.

> As soon as my sister asked me if I'd go with her when she was 18, I told my mum straight away. It's, like, because I was talking to her over Facebook I think it was, and my mum just walked in my room and said what I wanted for tea or something, and I

said, 'My sister's just asked me if I would go down with her when she's 18 and meet our birth parents', and Mum just automatically sat down on the bed and we started having a conversation about it. (Adopted young person, has face-to-face contact with sister, and also connects via Facebook)

And how important was your mum's attitude, how important was that?

I think it would be so difficult if she'd been, like, 'No, you can't'. Like when I told her, both my parents, that I wanted to find her [birth mother] they were so supportive, absolutely fantastic. I think if I didn't have that support, I think that's when you get people sneaking on Facebook and doing all these things behind their parents' backs. So it was really important to me that they were on board with it. (Adopted young person, contacted birth mother through Facebook)

You've mentioned Facebook contact. That's come into being since the last round of this project. So tell me how you use that with her.

Just occasionally send her messages, 'Are you OK?', just that really. Or send her photos or comment on her photos and stuff. Just as you would with anybody else really...It does give you a bit of an insight, like seeing what she's doing, but I don't make a point of always seeing what she's doing or saying 'hi'. (Birth mother, met adopted daughter as an adult)

Negative experiences of using social media

The use of social media driven by gaps in existing contact arrangements was sometimes helpful, but sometimes very unhelpful, especially where young people were unprepared and ill-equipped to cope. In some cases, Facebook had made it easy for young people to find their birth family members, often impulsively and when they were in an emotionally turbulent stage. The speed with which people could connect with birth family members allowed little time for thought or reflection. Young people did not always involve their adoptive parents in their social networking activities, for example, in one case an unhelpful reunion with the birth parent was hidden from the adoptive parents for a time.

So she'd then found [birth mother] on Facebook, added her and they'd started communicating on Facebook and then on webcam...so they were talking face-to-face. And...it was quite frightening how quick it was going. [Birth mother] refused to have any social work interaction within it...Because [birth mother] wasn't prepared, it was a disaster really in the end. (Adoptive mother)

[Birth mother] had come down, [adopted son] found her on Facebook...and they'd been phoning each other and she'd actually come down, met him by the shops, taken him into town for a coffee and he'd kept it from us for a year. He'd kept it from everybody, even the therapist. So understandably that had just thrown him over the edge as well, he couldn't cope with that at all. (Adoptive mother)

Summary

Examples of using social media were given by adopted young people, adoptive parents and birth relatives, and social media was used for three purposes: to gain information about another party, to communicate, and to search for and seek a reunion with another party. Where social media was used to supplement existing contact arrangements, and where young people had their adoptive parents' support, experiences were generally positive. Where social media was used to fill in gaps in existing contact, and where adoptive parents were not involved, outcomes were more likely to be negative.

Summary of findings and practice implications

Strengths of the research

- The same families have been followed over time, allowing for a longitudinal perspective on both adopted children's development and outcomes of post-adoption contact.
- The study has included multiple perspectives.
- The sample is fairly typical of children adopted in the UK today, where the majority are adopted from the care system when under the age of five.

Limitations of the research

- The sample is biased towards families with higher levels of contact, and where adoptive parents are communicatively open. The views of young people who have had no contact, and whose parents are less communicatively open, are likely to be underrepresented.
- Because the study is restricted to children adopted under the age of five, most of whom did not have established relationships with birth relatives, it is unlikely to fully reflect the views and experiences of families where children are older at the time of placement; contact may be more complex for such older children.

How were the adopted young people getting on in adolescence?

Key findings

About half of the young people were doing very well in terms of their overall development; the remainder had some problems and in some cases these were very worrying. Whether or not young people were doing well was affected by a range of factors both before and after placement, but contact with birth relatives did not seem to be an important factor in determining overall development.

Practice implications

- Many adopted children are likely to have ongoing needs that will require support. Adoption support plans should be realistic. Even when support needs are not immediately apparent, future needs should be anticipated, particularly in the child's teenage years. Specialist support services for families at this stage should be considered.
- Post-adoption contact should be considered on a case-by-case basis and should be grounded in a realistic understanding of the potential benefits and challenges, rather than un-evidenced assumptions about benefit or harm.

What types of openness have been experienced over the years?

Key findings

Overall, contact had continued to diminish over time, and one-third of young people were no longer in contact with any birth relatives. But in some cases contact had increased in late adolescence, usually at the young person's instigation. Direct contact arrangements seemed more likely to endure over time than indirect contact arrangements. The use of social networking websites for birth families and adoptive families to find out about or communicate with each other had emerged. This could be a helpful "add-on" to existing successful contact arrangements, but could be unhelpful when used as a means of filling gaps (for example, where adopted young people and birth relatives had no other easy means to find out about or get in touch with each other). Where adoptive parents maintained an open communication with their children about adoption and about the use of social networking websites, young people were better prepared to deal with any contact via social media.

Practice implications

- A proactive approach to supporting and reviewing contact is indicated.

- Information and support need to be available when contact stops.

- Where contact is mediated, communicate with all parties to review the plan as the young person approaches adulthood.

- Contact plans need to be realistic – how likely is it that they can be sustained over time? What support is required for this to happen?

- Support for adoptive parents in understanding the implications of social networking websites in adoption, and how to keep children safe, is key.

- Think carefully about any significant "gaps" for the child or for birth relatives; how can people's needs be met without resorting to social networking websites? This could be through ongoing contact, or where this is not possible or advisable, through other means of exchanging information.

What are the views of adopted young people, adoptive parents and birth relatives about the contact plans they have experienced?

Key findings

Views of contact varied from person to person, but where contact had been sustained, satisfaction was usually high. Successful contact arrangements seemed heavily dependent on the characteristics of the adoptive parents and birth relatives involved; as the children became adolescents, their influence on the dynamics of contact had increased.

For contact to work, it is important that adoptive parents and birth relatives respect each other's roles and family boundaries, have the capacity to focus on the needs of the adopted young person, and are willing to exchange information which gives birth relatives reassurance about how their child is getting on, and which allows the young person to gain a realistic understanding of their birth family.

Contact has emerged as not so much a succession of events (meetings or letters), but as a fluid process of people communicating with and relating to each other over a period of years.

Practice implications

- Be clear about the purpose of contact, e.g. is it to meet information needs? Is it to build or sustain a relationship? Is it to promote adoptive family communication about adoption? There needs to be shared understanding of and commitment to the purpose of contact.

- Support for contact needs to address issues of roles, boundaries and relationships – ideally at the planning stage, but also on an ongoing basis.

- As children grow up, their views and feelings about contact need to be taken into account.

- Some young people may not be ready to take responsibility for contact themselves at age 18, so support for mediated contact may need to continue beyond this age.

How were the adopted young people making sense of their adoptive identity?

Key findings

Young people varied in terms of how they were

making sense of their adoptive identity, but few were uninterested in adoption as a feature of their lives. Birth family contact appeared to have a role in promoting identity development both because it exposed the adoptive parents and child to information about the birth family, but also because it facilitated communication between the adopted young people and their adoptive parents, allowing young people to process their thoughts and feelings about the adoption.

Practice implications

- Ensure realistic background information is available to the adopted child and adoptive parents. This may need to be updated over the years.

- Support should be provided for adoptive parents in talking about difficult topics.

- Help people to use contact as a way to achieve effective information exchange.

- Support adoptive parents in using contact as a communication opportunity rather than just a meeting or letter.

- Support should be provided for birth relatives in answering children's questions; in deciding what to write in contact letters or letters for later life; and in helping grandparents to talk with the child about their birth parents' problems.

How open were adoptive parents in talking and thinking about adoption?

Key findings

This sample of adoptive parents was mostly very open in terms of adoption communication, probably more so than adoptive parents generally. Higher levels of birth family contact were linked to high levels of communication about adoption, as each promoted the other. Young people valued being able to talk to their parents about adoption. The adoption communication openness of adoptive parents has, throughout this study, emerged as an important aspect of adoptive parenting, whether or not children are able to have any actual contact with birth relatives.

Practice implications

- Consider adoption communication openness at the recruitment/assessment/preparation stage.

- Provide adoptive parents with ongoing support with communication with their children, especially at key stages where questions may arise, e.g. in middle childhood as awareness and understanding of adoption increases, and in adolescence as identity concerns may intensify.

How well were birth relatives doing in terms of their mental health and their acceptance of adoption?

Key findings

Many birth relatives had high levels of mental distress, and ongoing issues in coming to terms with the child's adoption. Positive experiences of contact with the adopted child were felt to mitigate their loss to some extent. Being able to have an ongoing role (the clarity of which seemed just as important as the nature or extent) in the child's life was something that birth relatives valued. Although contact had clearly worked better in cases where birth relatives could accept the child's adoption and promote their membership of the adoptive family, this study has also shown that how birth relatives feel about the child's adoption is not necessarily fixed, and that positive experiences of contact can help birth parents, grandparents and other relatives make sense of and cope with the loss of the child.

Practice implications

- Consider/assess birth relatives' potential to accept adoption/support the child after adoption. A sustained unsupportive position (especially anger and resistance) is a contraindication for contact; an accepting position is potentially a good resource for the adoptive family.

- Encourage birth relatives to use specialist birth relative adoption support services.

- Consider including the extended family in indirect and direct contact – especially when birth parents have problems that may make it hard for them to sustain contact or where there is a history of abuse and neglect.

- Ensure that birth relatives have support to maintain contact, e.g. help with writing letters, support at meetings.

- Help birth relatives to understand their potential role in the child's life after adoption and review this at intervals, e.g. when changes in contact occur, or when reunion is considered.

- Where birth relatives cannot have contact, plan to meet their needs for information about the child.

Publications from earlier stages of the study

Neil E (1999) 'The sibling relationships of adopted children and patterns of contact after adoption', in Mullender A (ed) *We are Family: Sibling relationships in placement and beyond*, London: BAAF

Neil E (2000) 'The reasons why young children are placed for adoption: findings from a recently placed sample and implications for future identity issues', *Child and Family Social Work*, 5:4, pp. 303–316

Neil E (2002) 'Contact after adoption: the role of agencies in making and supporting plans', *Adoption & Fostering*, 26:1, pp. 25–38

Neil E (2002) 'Managing face-to-face contact for young adopted children', in Argent H (ed) *Staying Connected: Managing contact arrangements in adoption*, London: BAAF

Neil E (2003) 'Understanding other people's perspectives: tasks for adopters in open adoptions', *Adoption Quarterly*, 6:3, pp. 3–30

Neil E (2003) 'Accepting the reality of adoption: birth relatives' experiences of face-to-face contact', *Adoption & Fostering*, 27:2, pp. 32–43

Neil E (2003) 'Contact after adoption: a research review', in Bainham M, Lindley B, Richards M and Trinder L (eds) *Children and their Families: Contact, rights and welfare*, Oxford: Richard Hart

Neil E, Beek M and Schofield G (2003) 'Thinking about and managing contact in permanent placements: the differences and similarities between adoptive parents and foster carers', *Clinical Child Psychology and Psychiatry*, 8:3, pp. 401–418.

Neil E (2004) 'The "Contact after Adoption" study: face-to-face contact', in Neil E and Howe D (eds) *Contact in Adoption and Permanent Foster Care: Research, theory and practice*, London: BAAF, pp. 65–84

Neil E (2004) 'The "Contact after Adoption" study: indirect contact and adoptive parents' communication about adoption', in Neil E and Howe D (eds) *Contact in Adoption and Permanent Foster Care: Research, theory and practice*, London: BAAF, pp. 46–64

Neil E and Howe D (2004) 'Conclusions: a transactional model for thinking about contact', in Neil E and Howe D (eds), *Contact in Adoption and Permanent Foster Care: Research, theory and practice*, London: BAAF, pp. 224–254

Young J and Neil E (2004) 'The "Contact after Adoption" study: the perspective of birth relatives after non-voluntary adoption', in Neil E and Howe D (eds), *Contact in Adoption and Permanent Foster Care: Research, theory and practice*, London: BAAF, pp. 85–104

Neil E (2007) 'Post-adoption contact and openness in adoptive parents' minds: consequences for children's development', *British Journal of Social Work – Advance Access*, available at: http://bjsw.oxfordjournals.org/content/39/1/5.full

Neil E (2007) 'Coming to terms with the loss of a child: the feelings of birth parents and grandparents about adoption and post-adoption contact', *Adoption Quarterly*, 10, pp. 1–23

Neil E (2009) 'The corresponding experiences of adoptive parents and birth relatives in open adoptions', in Wrobel G and Neil E (eds), *International Advances in Adoption Research for Practice*, Chichester: Wiley

Neil E (2012) 'Making sense of adoption: integration and differentiation from the perspectives of adopted children in middle childhood', *Children and Youth Services Review*, 34, pp. 409–416

Neil E, Beek M, Thoburn J, Schofield G and Ward E (2012), *Contact Arrangements for Adopted Children: What can be learned from research?*, Norwich: Centre for Research on the Child and Family, University of East Anglia

Neil E (2013) 'The mental distress of the birth relatives of adopted children: "disease" or "unease"?, *Health and Social Care in the Community*, 21:2, pp. 191–199

Other relevant adoption research publications from this research team

Cossar J and Neil E (2010) 'Supporting the birth relatives of adopted children: how accessible are services?', *British Journal of Social Work*, 40, pp. 1368–1386

Cossar J and Neil E (2013) 'Making sense of siblings: connections and severances in post-adoption contact', *Child & Family Social Work*, 18, pp. 67–76

Neil E (2008) 'Supporting post-adoption contact for children adopted from care: a study of social workers' attitudes', *Adoption Quarterly*, 10, pp. 3–28

Neil E (2010) 'The benefits and challenges of direct post-adoption contact: perspectives from adoptive parents and birth relatives', *Aloma*, 27, pp. 89–115

Neil E, Cossar J, Lorgelly P and Young J (2010) *Helping Birth Families: Services, costs and outcomes*, London: BAAF

Neil E, Cossar J, Lorgelly P and Young J (2011) *Supporting Contact after Adoption*, London: BAAF